Teaching Moral Values

Man and Religion Series
Part 7
Christianity and Our Culture

The Religious Education Press Ltd
a member of the Pergamon Group
Headington Hill Hall
Oxford

Teaching Moral Values

Lionel Ward

Lionel Ward
is Senior Lecturer in Education,
College of Domestic Arts
of South Wales and Monmouthshire,
Cardiff

Cover and Design
Keith Clements

57651

Man and Religion Series
General Editor Ronald Dingwall
Executive Editor Gordon K. Hawes MA BD
Art Director Keith Clements

The Religious Education Press Ltd
a member of the Pergamon Group
Oxford   London   Edinburgh
New York   Toronto   Sydney

First published 1969
© 1969 Lionel Ward

*1 008 0063764
0107861*

Made and Printed in Great Britain by
A Wheaton and Company
Exeter   Devon

L.O.C. 79–76290

08 006376 4

*170.7
WAR*

Contents

Introduction
Bibliography

1 **The Moral Problem**   1

The Philosophical Problem   1
The Psychological Problem   6
The Social Problem   8
Summary   15
Questions for Discussion
Bibliography   17

2 **Research Trends**   19

Measurement   19
Heredity and Environment   24
Mass Media   26
The School   29
Summary   30
Questions for Discussion
Bibliography   32

3 **Moral Values and Children**   36

The Primary School Child   36
The Secondary School Child   40
Summary   45
Questions for Discussion
Bibliography   47

4   **The Teacher and the School**   50

The Role of the Teacher   50
The Role of the School   56
Summary   65
Questions for Discussion
Bibliography   67

Introduction

The natural reaction of anyone reading the title of this book is to   *1*
ask, "How can you **teach moral values**?" One has to confess
that this question may not be a request for information but an
implied criticism of the whole basis of moral education. What a
moral education is, and how it is achieved, are problems which
are basically insoluble so long as we differ in our interpretation
of what is moral, or in the reasons for erecting a system of morality
and attempting to make others adhere to it. These questions raise
the most profound issues of moral philosophy, social psychology
and law which are beyond the scope of a short work like this and
have been expertly dealt with elsewhere (2) (5) (9) (12).

How many moral judgments do we make in a day? On how   *2*
many issues can we make moral judgments? The answer to these
questions is probably that we do not know. Most of our moral
decisions are silent and personal; we do not all carry banners to
demonstrate our major convictions. Those who do are clearly
anxious to convince themselves of their strength of belief and
encourage that belief in others. Whether the issues be the great
ones of freedom of thought, racial harmony or poverty, or whether
they are concerned with speed-limits, lowflying aircraft, or even
comments on fashion or pop-music—they all rest on one's view
of human nature. These issues provide endless material for
discussion and argument and for varying human conduct.

3   It is perhaps the apparent change in values and conduct that is responsible for the renewed interest in moral education in the last decade or so. A former Minister of Education selected this theme for an article in **Education for Teaching,** thus indicating a concern for an educational subject that is very far removed from the ordinary political and administrative routine which forms the bulk of his work (3). This concern soon after led Christians and humanists to join together in the desire to see moral education given a more definitely considered place in the life of the school (13). They recognized the need for honesty and frank discussion at all levels, for moral education to permeate throughout rather than figure in a timetable, and for neutrality—which, as Halsey (8) has said, is hardly more moral than accepting rules impersonally—to be discouraged. The permissive spirit has operated for some time, and not always to our disadvantage, but it is worth reminding ourselves of the conservative tradition that lies at the heart of every society, and that in this sense

> 'moral education is a matter of initiating others into traditions and into procedures for revising and applying them' (11).

4   As an agent of this tradition the teacher cannot escape this responsibility which arises either within or outside the framework of the subject being taught. Frequently the latter is the case, but as Vick (8) has pointed out, even in science, where morality does not seem to figure prominently, the teaching of values is possible: the good scientist has standards, wishes to be free of pressures, and wants to work creatively, often with others.

5   The interesting work of the Farmington Trust Research Unit has already resulted in a detailed work on the subject of Moral Education which, despite its title, is more than is customarily regarded as an introduction (12). This description, however, is intended to show that more work will follow. Anyone undertaking a serious study of the subject will find the book indispensible,

although challenging. In addition there are numerous further sources, to which reference has been made in the text of the present book; a study of these sources, which are listed at the end of each chapter, will contribute to a further understanding of the matter in hand.

In chapter **1** a survey is made of the various problems associated with moral education—the difficulties one is faced with in assuming a moral standpoint, detecting one in others, and attempting to influence others. The aim of chapter **2** is to provide a guide to research which, although it may not always suggest complete and permanent answers to many of our queries, is as much as human ingenuity has yet achieved. Perhaps the concern which research workers have shown for the subject may persuade their critics in the teaching profession to concede that not all research is unrealistic, and encourage those teachers with an interest and aptitude to undertake some research for themselves (4). During his training the student-teacher has to make a major adjustment: he must transfer his feelings of identification with the interests of the children to those of the teacher he is about to become. Nevertheless he must retain his insight into, and sympathy with, the ideals and aspirations of the children. The student may not always remember what kind of moral outlook is typical of any particular age-range, and although studying this from a book is only part of the answer, some attempt to describe the various outlooks is made in chapter **3**. In this chapter objections can be expressed to abstractions such as 'the primary school child' and some allowance has to be made for the infinite variability of attitudes. The final chapter attempts to show the kind of school atmosphere and teacher-pupil relationship which appear to offer the greatest hope for moral education. The major conclusion is that Vidler and Eppel (8) are right when they say a morality of contsraint and inhibition is not enough.

The major objection, as has already been suggested, may be

6

7

to the whole concept of **teaching moral values**. Bearing in mind that teaching is losing its meaning of 'indoctrination or formal instruction,' there is still a place for '**teaching moral values**.' Jocelyn Peters (10) puts it very concisely:

> 'The growth of morality is a complex affair belonging to both the realms of identification and conflict in early childhood and to the conscious character training in home and school in later years. To be the protagonist of the former it is not necessary to neglect the importance of the latter.'

The modern world is complex and

> 'requires an increasing proportion of intelligently responsible people'

and yet it

> 'is full of influences hostile to intelligent responsibility' (6).

As Marjorie Reeves (8) has said, the educator must bring the child up against hard moral decisions. Quoting Robert Bolt, she shows the attraction of the moral commitment exemplified in the life of Thomas More (1). Here was a man who, though he

> 'gratefully accepted the shelter of his society',

was prepared to be

> 'thrust out into the terrifying cosmos'.

We all have an ultimate loyalty but few of us are put to the ultimate test; we are in a more complex situation than that in which More found himself for we have to make

> 'the authoritative transmission of a received tradition . . . give way to the open search for living truth'. (7).

Bibliography

(1)
Bolt, R. **A Man for All Seasons.**
London: Heinemann, 1960.

(2)
Devlin, P. **The Enforcement of Morals.**
London: Oxford University Press, 1965.

(3)
Eccles, D. **Values.**
Education for Teaching, November, 1961, 6–7.

(4)
Evans, K. M. **Planning Small-Scale Research.**
*National Foundation for Educational Research,
1968.*

(5)
Hare, R. M. **Freedom and Reason.**
London : Oxford University Press, 1963.

(6)
Jeffreys, M. V. C. **Personal Values in the Modern World.**
Penguin Books, 1966.

(7)
Loukes, H. **New Ground in Christian Education.**
London: S.C.M. Press, 1965.

(8)
Niblett, W. R. (ed) **Moral Education in a Changing Society.**
London: Faber and Faber, 1963.
Halsey, A. H. The Sociology of Moral Education.
Peters, R. S. Reason and Habit: The paradox of Moral
Education.
Vick, F. A. Science and its Standards.

Vidler, A. R.   Religious Belief Today and its Moral Derivatives.

Winnicott, D. W.   The Young Child at Home and at School.

Eppel, E. M.   The Adolescent and Changing Moral Standards.

Loukes, H.   Responsibility and Irresponsibility in Adolescents.

Reeves, M. E.   Moral Education in Early Maturity.

(9)

Nowell-Smith, P.   **Ethics.**
Penguin Books, 1954.

(10)

Peters, J.   **Growing-Up World.**
London: Longmans, 1966.

(11)

Peters, R. S   **Moral Education and the Psychology of Character.**
A paper read at the Conference organized by the Harvard Graduate School of Education, May, 1961.

(12)

Wilson, J.   **Introduction to Moral Education.**
Williams, N.   *Penguin Books, 1968.*
Sugarman, B.

(13)

Religious and Moral Education—Some Proposals for County Schools by a Group of Christians and Humanists.
Leicester: Blackfriars Press, 1965.

The Moral Problem 1

The Philosophical Problem

In 1859, in his famous book **On Liberty** John Stuart Mill wrote, **1.***1*

> 'The only freedom which deserves the name, is that of
> pursuing our own good in our own way, so long as we
> do not attempt to deprive others of theirs, or impede
> their efforts to obtain it . . . . Mankind are greater
> gainers by suffering each other to live as seems good to
> themselves, than by compelling each to live as seems
> good to the rest.'

Mill is the parent of individualism, an important factor in
liberalism which, as Bertrand Russell has said, is the attempt to
escape from the endless oscillation between the demands of social
cohesion and the conditions necessary for personal independence
(9).

How displeased Mill would now be at the growth of his
offspring it is difficult to tell, but since he lived within the
Victorian moral code there is little doubt that he would be
alarmed at the distortion and popularization of his views a
century later. For example, existentialism, which owes a good
deal to Mill's individualism, asserts that there are no objective
universal values, and that the individual has to create his own
values through action and living life to the full. When pressed,

holders of this opinion will concede that there is a necessity to avoid hurting others in the process, but often show little awareness of the fact that hardly any action one does is completely devoid of significance for others.

1.2   The fundamental problem about basing one's moral values on individualism, whether it be Mill's or a form or extension of it, is that we are accepting too readily a solution that was found intellectually acceptable a century ago, but is to some extent at odds with modern development. Individualism is the philosophical basis of liberalism but, as MacIntyre (4) points out, whereas the Victorians were entering liberalism, we are leaving it. The change from individualism to collectivism has profoundly altered the way in which we approach philosophy, economics and other comparatively new subjects like sociology and sociometry where the main interest is in the **group** or the influence of the **group** on the **individual**. Discussion of the **individual** as an isolated phenomenon rarely takes place in serious abstract investigation.

If at first sight this appears to conflict with centuries of classical, Christian and humanist concern for the individual, it should be remembered that what is being examined is the formal discussion of problems rather than practical action to solve them. This explains the apparent paradox of a Welfare State which has grown in an age when the abstract argument is no longer conducted in purely individualist terms, but where the individual is cared for more than ever. In fact, in the view of Victorian liberals the present care for the individual would be regarded as excessive.

1.3   Another problem which we do not have in common with Mill is that, unlike him, we neither share in a general moral consensus nor possess an essential optimism. Mill accepted the general moral principles of the time, even though he would have argued that the commonly accepted religious sanction for them was not a valid one. His optimism came from his study of the sociology of Comte, just as Kant derived his optimism from the

Enlightenment, which involved a belief in the ability of man through his reason to conquer all human problems. We have lost much of this capacity for optimism, and those who are most anxious about the basis of morality are those who should have authority in moral teaching. Those who show no such anxiety owe their peace of mind to several factors: complete indifference, a refusal to recognise any problem, or a willingness to accept without question religious, dogmatic sanctions. The extent to which these sanctions can be applied rationally and consistently, provides the justification for the possession and enforcement of moral values by law or persuasion.

Mill himself recognized the limits of *laissez-faire* doctrine, for, **1.4** to use the economic language from which it originated, it works only where the consumer is an adequate judge of the product. Because the child is not in a good position to judge the merits of different values, the teacher has to take a part in encouraging adherence to those principles which his experience has taught him are representative of society at its best. In the absence of an authoritative source of information on the nature of those principles—and in many Western countries the teacher is given considerable latitude in deciding for himself—the teacher has to deduce his standpoint from his own interaction with society. As Jacques Maritain, in **Education at the Crossroads**, has said:

'The aim of education . . . is to guide man in the evolving dynamism through which he shapes himself as a human person—armed with knowledge, strength of judgment, and moral virtue—while at the same time conveying to him the spiritual heritage of the nation and the civilization in which he is involved'.

This freedom is in the hands of a profession, the status of **1.5** which is often said to be low. The question therefore arises whether it was given out of respect for the profession, or for some other reason—because of an underestimation of the power of teachers to influence the minds of the young. If, as seems likely, academic merit has been emphasized, to some extent at the expense of moral maturity, it is a reflection of changes in our thinking about what constitutes a good teacher, and a recognition of the great difficulty in agreeing on sound moral attitudes and measuring them accurately.

1.6   When we say that it is an important duty of the teacher to **teach moral values** we usually mean one of two things. Firstly, remembering that the child must take a place in the community, we attempt to bring about some conformity to the conventional standards of society. Secondly, we attempt to help the child to make all his values consistent and to develop a stable element in his personality. Increasing attention has been directed to the fact that personal moral education must be discussed in either its cognitive aspect (the ability to perceive moral issues) or its emotional one (where the reaction is affected by the extent to which norms are violated). Learning values is a process sustained by the interaction of groups and motivated by social sanctions. Expectations are established concerning the way a member ought to behave, and the behaviour which either exerts or responds to pressures designed to induce conformity has been called **normative behaviour**. So the standards or principles enforced by social pressures have been called **norms**.

1.7   The real purpose of moral education may be said to be the attempt to strike the balance between its personal and social aspects. Unless one is at war with the values of one's society, it is likely that one will identify oneself to some extent with the values of that society, so far as it is possible to ascertain them. Any difficulties that arise do so for reasons other than a conviction that they are on balance the best in the circumstances. Having convinced himself of the need to teach certain values, the teacher is often driven to take up an authoritative position. Wilson (13) has suggested the limits to which one ought to go in subordinating personal wills to the dictates of society. He says that our mandate over children includes the right to condition to some extent and use force or compulsion, but indoctrination should be avoided. The distinction drawn between conditioning and indoctrination is that the former involves giving a person a fear and repulsion concerning something one considers undesirable, whereas indoctrination is not a direct overriding of the will, but the act of persuading a person he has freely accepted a value, when in fact his will and reason have been temporarily put to sleep.

Much attention has recently been directed to the problem of achieving objective and universal standards by which morality can be judged (13). It is impossible to prove that one religion or code of ethics is superior to another, for unlike mathematics and science there is no objective standard which has universal validity. The predicament then arises that there is a reluctance to make the value-judgment which establishes which principles or actions are considered desirable. We may have to choose an authority for our actions, for there is no sense in considering morals in a vacuum. Much of the recent discussion of moral education has been philosophic and formal—that is devoid of content—and is intent on searching for a single body of principles for discriminating between moral codes which could be discovered, and ought, when formulated, to have the authority that scientific method possesses. MacIntyre (5) comments that moralities vary, just as concepts of morality vary, and it is still open to question whether **1.8**

> 'we can find a true common subject matter for intellectual inquiry under the rubric "moral education"'.

To the majority of people the philosophical problem is a barren controversy, and as Loukes (3) says, **1.9**

> 'the heart of morality is not in abstract moral theory: it is a sense of common kinship, an understanding of the feelings and needs of other people. It begins when we first discover another person, feel him to be real,

and recognise that his very existence makes demands
on us.'

This statement links well with certain moral components suggested
by Wilson (13) who points out that what is needed is an awareness
of the feelings of others, an accurate knowledge of the facts of the
situation, an ability to formulate principles rationally and apply
them consistently in one's life.

The Psychological Problem

1.*10*   Values are usually defined as more or less stable patterns
around an object. Even after we agree on what, in any situation,
is 'moral,' there are difficulties which are encountered in the field
of attitude-testing. Assessment and measurement are central to
the study of the psychology of education, but some areas—the
testing of intelligence and personality, for example—have
developed more quickly than the study of moral attitudes. The
reason for this must lie outside the problems of definition and
measurement which affect all equally. Perhaps the explanation
lies in the fact that problems of educational selection and psych-
iatric study have put great pressure on the search for reliable
tools of analysis. Since Binet's day there has been an increasing
need for a method of isolating those who might benefit from a
particular kind of education. Personality tests were developed
at first as a by-product of work in psychiatry, and then were
applied in education to investigate the reasons for success and
failure among pupils.

1.*11*   In measuring moral attitudes we are lucky if we get completely honest answers, for the testee is tempted to give a more
acceptable answer than usual in order to present a good picture
of himself. Even this subterfuge, of course, shows some recognition

of standards, but what is still not known is the size of the conscious shift of attitude. This action, which is not confined to children, has been described, however, as

> 'the momentary desire to pronounce moral precepts
> pleasing to the adult' (7).

This tendency is most obvious where the moral issue is not hidden, and the more successful tests give the impression of testing completely different qualities. Attempts to clarify an opinion by a re-examination might lead to second thoughts, which are seldom more genuine than first ones, and certainly not as spontaneous. The very fact of a re-examination suggests a need for the person to change his attitude.

Once we have the information we know what the person tested thinks in relation to the test he has been given, and can place his answers on a scale, but there is no way of assessing objectively the 'correctness' of his responses. This situation encourages the use of words like 'untypical' rather than words like 'bad', and a value-judgment has to be made. Since attitudes are constantly changing, one can never regard them as a permanent expression of the personality of the person, although moral attitudes have a life which is usually longer than that of factual information. Vernon (10) has suggested that below the mental age of 12 years the testing of attitudes may be untrustworthy, and in terms of absolute accuracy of assessment at any age, any discrepancy between the expressed opinion and the real opinion has to be accepted.

Values may or may not affect behaviour in any situation, **1.***12* but a conflict of values invariably induces unfavourable behaviour unless the child is introduced to the fact that all men do not share the same values, and some knowledge of the working of his own value-system is gained. Thus the description of the building up of values is usually as follows: an honest child is praised, and because he likes praise he considers it wise to be honest. As a result of being honest in various situations he develops a generalized concept of honesty, which will constantly be modified to allow for changing circumstances. In this process he may acquire an 'ideal', wishing to imitate him, and finally developing generalized moral principles. The human reaction to impossibly difficult situations is to compromise with them, but the extent to which one keeps to a moral position has been linked with the possession of 'impulse judgment'. This has been defined as the ability to weigh up immediate and possible future satisfaction and decide which is more desirable, or in other terms as the willingness to forego immediate gains in order to achieve a remote but more rewarding gain (6) (11).

1.*13*   Any more precise definition of the morality of an attitude is unlikely, and moral development may be a complex of factors. Even if these could be isolated there would be no excuse for ignoring the irrational element in moral values. Few people have a rational code of values, and fewer still apply them consistently. Where there is calculation it usually does not extend beyond the effect an attitude or action may have on one's self or one's relations with others. Consistency, if it comes, may well be the result of habit, hardly related to any conscious scheme. Nevertheless the attempt to make moral values and behaviour more rational and consistent should be made, if only because it reduces tension in a person when he can justify his actions in retrospect in rational terms.

The Social Problem

1.*14*   In any society a man is 'moral' if in thought and action he gives the appearance of adhering to those standards which his society has evolved as being just and right. In common usage the word 'moral' is identified with sexual ideals, but there is no reason why the growing tendency to talk of the 'morality' of warfare, racial discrimination and other evils should not be continued. In contrast, with the exception of Gesell (2), for example, the word 'ethical' has had strong overtones of business and professional standards. The more these words become interchangeable, the greater progress we shall be making towards the realisation that all problems described as ethical and moral have their origin and solution in the way society regards its individual members, and the relationships between the members of society.

Only when we have clearly established what the aims of **1.***15* society are can we intelligently and consciously teach those values which are necessary for the achievement of those goals which are generally approved. Where do we look for the enunciation of those goals by those with sufficient perception and literacy—and the assent of the vast majority of people—which would justify the assumption that these are the values most widely respected? There is, of course, no single authoritative source for deciding the values of our present society, and the teacher, in order to fulfil his role adequately, has to be sufficiently involved in society, and critical of it, to preserve a balanced view of the competing and conflicting aims which society embodies. If there were objective standards of morality, society would have no problem other than deciding how to enforce them, or recognizing the failure of people to live up to them.

Any teacher, when considering the climate or atmosphere **1.***16* which he thinks desirable for a school, has to consider the school as a part of society, for there is a constant danger that the school will demand values that are impossibly rigid or in conflict with those of society at large. Unless the school can encourage discrimination the child will be unprepared for the transition to life in industry, commerce or higher education, where compromise and individual interpretation of the situation are necessary. This lack of realism, which the young believe is characteristic of many educational institutions, is one cause of student unrest, together with the refusal of those in authority to allow discussion of issues of common interest.

1.17   Socially, one of the great intangibles is the moral climate of the country or district in which one resides, and the differences to be observed operate as powerfully between areas or regions of a country as they do between one country and another. Thus the inhabitants of a Welsh or Scottish village will have moral values very different from the mass of Londoners, while the values of Londoners will differ from those of other city-dwellers on the Continent. The uniqueness of every society is the outcome of political, religious and other circumstances, and are the factors which every teacher learns to understand, and usually respect, when he enters an unfamiliar region for the first time.

1.18   In a liberal democracy no church or political party has the dominance which allows it to assert control over the moral values of the people. In contrast, totalitarian states erect alternative value-systems, making loyalty to the state take precedence in many areas over the exercise of conscience, and regulating the lives of people, even in matters of dress. One of the most encouraging signs in recent times has been the reluctance, even of those who have lived all their lives in totalitarian regimes, to accept regimes which do not allow the maximum freedom of choice of values. The difficulty which faces all societies is that there may be dissatisfaction with them, especially among students; but the alternatives suggested are largely impracticable, and those who suggest the new values lack the ability, or power, to create a new society based on the new values. Unless this revolutionary potential can be directed into productive and creative channels the result is likely to be social chaos.

1.19   In the last century, concern for moral education took the form of training 'Christian gentlemen' in the prosperous classes, and giving moral indoctrination to the masses. The changes which have since led to the so-called 'permissive society' are described elsewhere (12). The argument runs that, as there are no absolute and universal moral standards, and as inhibiting the individual is harmful, society should exert as little pressure as possible on its members to conform to values which are considered out-dated. The question of the absence of objective standards has been considered, and the mistaken view that Freud's concept of repression meant inhibiting—and not the exclusion of painful and unpleasant material from consciousness—is the other argument often heard.

Now that secondary education for all has been achieved, **1.**20 attention has been directed increasingly to the content and techniques of education. Both are relevant, for one would not vitiate the good work that can be achieved by new material by oppressive or tedious methods. Many questions need to be answered. What should one teach in order to promote moral development? In what ways can various subjects assist this? What limits of decency and good taste are there in selecting material to show the more unpleasant parts of human nature? What are the techniques which are most successful in encouraging healthy moral development?

These concerns have been forced upon us by the pace of **1.**21 social change. A decline, or at least a change, in the nature of parental authority is often spoken about. Many parents exercise a control as effective as in the past, but it is unlikely to be based on such authoritarian grounds as used to be the case. Mutual co-operation and rational discussion play a large part in family relationships, but the process, it is often argued, can be taken too far. Parents and children have definite roles to play, and it is easy to forget the limitations of reason and experience which the child has, and his need for, and expectation of, definite guidance. The abdication of parental authority, so far as it exists, may be the result not merely of neglect, but of an unwillingness to enforce standards which are not generally accepted, and an unwillingness or inability to engage in rational discussion with articulate and well-educated children. In the last resort, there is a reluctance to justify action simply on the grounds of parental authority without discussion, where through the immaturity of the child discussion is considered pointless. The desirability of parental meetings, possibly arranged through schools, where consistent and widely accepted standards can be established, is very obvious.

1.22 The increase in the number of working mothers is often pointed to as the reason for the removal from the home, often at important points in the day, of a strong force in moral education. Where, as in the Soviet Union, play-centres exist for the children thus deprived, some compensation can be found, and there is the additional social training which has been demanded for many years. In the changing role of women in society, some blurring of the respective functions of men and women has occurred. The father is often no longer the authoritative figure, and the mother often lacks the time to be the source of the most enduring moral values. Undoubtedly, exceptional families survive this, and derive strength from the increase in cooperation which the mother's extra responsibilities force upon them.

1.23 The traditional social agencies of moral guidance, the Church and the school, have had their functions and responsibilities altered by changes in the intellectual climate, and the decline in church attendance has placed a greater burden upon the schools. The success of the Church in establishing its moral leadership has always borne some relationship to its ability to form a physical or spiritual community in which it is a major leader of opinion. A striking example of this in modern times has been the success of certain churches on new housing estates, where, by becoming a significant element in the social life of the community, the moral values which the church represents can be perpetuated.

Similarly, the atmosphere in our schools has changed radically, and with the disappearance of authoritarian methods there has been an increased response on the part of the child to act well. The establishment of a cooperative spirit in a school is not easy, for at first some direction is essential. The increasing physical and intellectual maturity demand a new approach to pupils which older teachers find hard to adopt, and the raising of the school-leaving age to 16 will need to be accompanied by a renewed attention to the problem. Both personal and civic responsibilities are being forced on the adolescent earlier than ever, partly by his earlier physical maturity, and partly by the intention to give the vote at an earlier age.

The effect on the young of exposure to mass media has **1.**24 worried many, and not only those who have campaigned against what they regard as immoral programmes or films. David Holbrook in **The Secret Places** condemns mass media for the exploitation of youthful imagination, with 'teen' magazines, 'constructed ideals', and 'false thrills'. Children are incapable as a result of dealing creatively with the great things of life and their own experience. Concern that television blurs reality and fiction and appears to condone or be neutral concerning undesirable conduct may be unwarranted. Reality itself may be unpleasant, and the question has to be asked whether material is intended to inform, amend, entertain or stimulate emotions. Television brings home the great suffering, for example, endured by ordinary people in times of war, and the minute examination of this suffering may perhaps only be justified by the effect it has in changing attitudes in a way that will reduce the prospect of future suffering and grief. Even the sincere and intelligent programme or film may be morally or aesthetically unacceptable to many, but the responsibility for deciding whether such material should be seen rests, in the case of children at least, with their parents.

The most effective basis, rationally and emotionally, for **1.**25

moral education is a religious one, as there is in Christianity a dogmatic basis which can be rationally discussed and which gives considerable emotional satisfaction. The neutral, undenominational religious instruction originating in the Cowper-Temple section of the 1870 Education Act tended to emasculate the subject; and confusion among Christians and the popular demand for simple Biblical knowledge or comparative religion have only further clouded the issue. To secularists, too firm an insistence on knowing that a course of action is pleasing to God opens a person to the charge of arrogance, but the attempts of humanists to found a morality based on human nature lack universality, as in different cultures different qualities are considered moral. The good general principle of reciprocity (or the Golden Rule) breaks down because, although one may wish to treat others as one would wish to be treated, even in the most civilised countries, national sovereignty prevents this. Isolating people of the past as examples of virtue or evil has its limitations; allowance has to be made for their very different historical circumstances and moral assumptions, and it must be agreed that great people have accepted what to us is unacceptable. Aristotle accepted slavery and Luther urged the slaughter of the peasants in 1525!

The dogmatic basis which Christianity could provide is no longer insisted on with the rigidity which characterised the past, and the next stage could be the removal of overt religious influence in schools by the abolition of compulsory religious teaching and observance. It has been argued with great logic that once the State recognises it has no religion, its refusal to enforce Christian beliefs removes its right to enforce specifically Christian morals (1).

1.26   The common core of all religions is a common admiration of mercy, courage, loyalty and justice, besides emphasising man's duty to the young and the old, and the mutual responsibilities of parent and child. To this one may add the argument that there is a 'moral route to theistic belief' (8).

This is

> 'that the ultimate, unconditional, absolute, underived
> and transcendent attributes of the values we encounter
> in experience reflect and point to their ground in an
> ultimate, unconditional, absolute, underived and trans-
> cendent God.'

This does not bring us entirely to the personal God of Christian belief, but moral experience provides the 'germ' of religious faith which requires for its germination the atmosphere of revelation and the Church.

Summary

1.*1*–**1.***7*

The individualist approach to morals is inadequate, for it neglects the demands of society. The *laissez-faire* theory is equally inadequate, especially for those who are too young to be competent judges, and an increasingly complex society has to evolve complicated and sophisticated techniques of assuring that its members live with sufficient regard for their fellows. This is not to undervalue the individual, since Western tradition, based among other things on the classical, Christian and liberal ideals, insists that the individual should play an important role in society. The search for universal, objective standards by which moral values may be established, would, if successful, greatly assist in moral education, though some express scepticism as to the possibilities of success.

1.*8*–**1.***13*

Values are difficult to measure, partly because they are constantly changing, and partly because the person tested does not always give the true picture of himself and his values. In order to establish whether a value is 'good' or 'bad', a value-judgment has to be made. The behaviourist approach stresses the element of conditioning in learning values, though some suggest one is born with at least the capacity for the operation of conscience. Frequently, acquiring moral standards is the process by which ideal persons are selected and their characters and deeds emulated. There is an irrational, and often inconsistent, element in morality; moral development may not be one, but a complex of factors.

1.*14*–**1.***26*

Moral standards and values are largely socially determined, and though they originate in society, there is no single authoritative source for them. Each community has a moral climate which usually differs from that of most other communities. A major part in erecting value-systems can be played by the State or Church. Socially there is less distinction between the classes as to the kind of moral education they require, and now that secondary education for all has been achieved, the time may have come for looking afresh at moral education. Changes in the nature of authority—of State, Church, parent and teacher—make this urgent. The earlier physical maturing of children, their exposure to more numerous and potent influences, and the removal of the dogmatic basis of Christian teaching, remind us of the need to think anew of the essential values which we wish the child to learn. In this the gap between the Christian and the humanist may not be as great as one might imagine.

Questions for Discussion

1. To what extent are moral values the most important thing one can teach?

2. What do you understand by the term 'moral education' and what link is there with religious education?

3. What are the authorities on which one may base a moral choice or action, and what are the strength and weaknesses of those authorities?

4. How can we know when other people are acting morally?

5. Are the pressures on an individual to think and act in a certain way too great or too small?

Bibliography

(1)
Devlin, P. **The Enforcement of Morals.**
London: Oxford University Press, 1965.

(2)
Gesell, A. **Youth: the Years from Ten to Sixteen.**
London: Hamish Hamilton, 1956.

(3)
Loukes, H. **The Teaching of Religion and Morals**
in Techniques of Teaching,
ed. A. D. C. Peterson. Oxford: Pergamon
Press, 1965.

(4)
MacIntyre, A. **What is Truth in Morals?**
New Society, June 11, 1964.

(5)
MacIntyre, A. *Review of* **Introduction to Moral**
Education.
New Society, February 29, 1968.

(6)
Maller, J. B. **General and Specific Factors in**
Character.
J. Soc. Psychol., 5, 97–102, 1934.

(7)
Piaget, J. **The Moral Judgement of the Child.**
London: Routledge, 1932.

(8)
Richmond, J. **Faith and Philosophy.**
London: Hodder and Stoughton, 1966.

(9)

Russell, B. **History of Western Philosophy.**
London: George Allen and Unwin, 1946.

(10)

Vernon, P. E. **Personality Tests and Assessments.**
London: Methuen, 1964.

(11)

Washburne, J. N. **Definitions in Character Measurement.**
J. Soc. Psychol. 2, 114–19, 1931.

(12)

Whitely, C. H. **The Permissive Society.**
Whitely, W. M. *London: Methuen, 1964.*

(13)

Wilson, J. **Introduction to Moral Education.**
Williams, N. *Penguin Books, 1968.*
Sugarman, B.

Measurement

Although the research worker has long been active in the field of   **2.***1*
moral education, the results of his work have not provided for the
teacher a sufficiently objective standard of measuring moral
maturity. Some of the reasons for this failure, especially the
difficulty of defining 'moral maturity', have already been considered. For at least half a century it has been argued that it
might be possible to measure the moral values of the child by
testing his judgments in various situations. The assumption, which
will be examined critically later, was that one can detect the fact
that a child who pronounces 'correctly' on the values of actions he
has been told about is, on the whole, a morally better person than
one whose judgment is less acute (7).

One of the earliest and most influential attempts to detect a   **2.***2*
pattern in the development of children's moral ideas was the
schema suggested by Piaget (25). By studying children's attitudes
to the game of marbles, and learning to play himself, Piaget
claimed that it revealed the truth that

> 'all morality consists in a system of rules, and the essence
> of all morality is to be sought for in the respect which
> the individual acquires for these rules.'

This led him to state that

'most of the moral rules which the child learns to respect
he receives from adults, which means that he receives
them after they have been fully elaborated, not in relation to him as they are needed, but once and for all
and through in uninterrupted succession of earlier
adult generations.'

By studying children's attitudes to adult authority as
revealed in stories, two main trends were discerned. The first
attitude was based on moral realism, or the

'tendency which the child has to regard duty and the
value attaching to it as self-subsistent and independent
of mind, as imposing itself regardless of the circumstances in which the individual may find himself.'

This attitude has three characteristics, one of which is that obeying the rules is important; the view of duty involves the mind
being subjected to a law other than reason. Thus

'any act that shows obedience to a rule or even to an
adult, regardless of what he may command, is good;
any act that does not conform is bad. A rule is, therefore, not in any way something elaborated, or even
judged and interpreted by the mind; it is given as such,
ready made and external to the mind. It is also con-
ceived of as revealed by the adult and imposed by him.
The good, therefore, is rigidly defined by obedience.'

Moral realism implies an observation of the letter rather than
the spirit of the law, no account being taken of the possible
consequences of such action.

Piaget further suggested that as the child grows up he moves
from an attitude based on moral realism to one based on equality.
This means that the intentions behind the act become important,
and that it is not considered wrong to have a will of one's own.
This is not to say that parental influence is unimportant at this
stage for, as Piaget says,

'it is often at the expense of the adult, and not because of
him, that the notions of just and unjust find their way
into the youthful mind.'

A sense of justice, though affected by adult example, grows out
of the mutual respect and solidarity among children themselves.
For

'morality pre-supposes the existence of rules which
transcend the individual, and these rules could only
develop through contact with other people.'

It is undeniably valuable to understand the stages through **2.***3*
which the child must pass in his moral development, but what is
really needed, as Gesell (11) has pointed out, is the establishment
of **norms** for ethical or moral attitudes. Gesell has already
started this process by describing the values he considered typical
of each year throughout the whole school. There is much to be
said for understanding the viewpoints of each year, although it is
open to the criticism that to distinguish so finely is not really a
justifiable exercise. The search for clear norms may be doomed
to failure, but it is often possible to detect general patterns of
thought at various stages in school life.

The major development for the child, if the stages of moral **2.***4*
realism and equality are accepted, is the change from the one
stage to the other. Although these concepts had not been devised
at the time, Macaulay and Watkins (21) made a similar point when
they suggested that the break with conventional morality occurs
around 14 years of age, when, with girls at least, a sense of responsibility to one's fellows begins to grow. The special emphasis on
girls may well be accounted for by earlier physical and emotional
maturity, both of which are related to moral development. It is
true that the whole study was based on American culture in the
1920's and its relevance for the present day is to some extent
limited. Trends among boys of 12 to 15 revealed by attitude-
scales have shown that there is a decrease in honesty, reflecting

the growth of unfavourable attitudes (2) (8). The reason for this may be that the ability to apply moral principles to an increasing range of conflicting life-situations is quite undeveloped at 16 years. Even mature and intelligent adults have standards that are a complex mixture of the mature and immature, and there is often little to distinguish their attitudes to life-situations from those of adolescents (30).

2.5   The extent to which intelligence affects moral judgment and growth is of obvious interest, and seems to depend on whether the cognitive or emotional aspect is being stressed. Edwards (8), in a study of secondary modern school boys, found only a slight correlation between scores in attitude-scale and intelligence. Peel's investigations indicate that both chronological age and mental age are significantly related to moral judgment up to $9\frac{1}{2}$ years, but that from then until 11 years the significance of mental age is reduced as chronological age assumes more importance. Given sufficient intelligence to understand the moral issue and to indicate one's position in relation to it, the importance of mental age seems to decrease throughout adolescence (14).

2.6   Imprecise concepts have been the major reason for the lack of unanimity among research workers, and even Piaget has had his critics. Criticism has been made of his juxtaposition of psychological and sociological terms and the vagueness of concepts employed (13). Some have even failed to detect the operation of his principles of moral realism and equality at the ages they are supposed to have relevance (4). He has also been accused of underestimating the emotional richness and complexity of the child under two or three years (18). Although the importance of children's groups for the development of moral values is paramount, there is probably room for more adult influence than Piaget conceded. Finally, cognitive moral development may not be one factor but a number of factors (22).

2.7   An interesting schema which represents an advance on that of Piaget has been presented by Kohlberg (19):

Stage 1 **Premoral**
    Type 1 Punishment and obedience orientation
    Type 2 Naive instrumental hedonism
Stage 2 **Morality of Conventional Role—Conformity.**
    Type 3 Maintaining good relations and approval
    Type 4 Authority maintaining morality
Stage 3 **Morality of Self-Accepted Moral Principles.**
    Type 5 Contract—individual rights and democratic laws
    Type 6 Morality of individual conscience.

It is interesting to note the emphasis on a pre-moral stage where the principles of morality do not really apply, and where the types are distinguished by a conditioning, either through traditional punishment or using inducements. The second stage (of conformity) elaborates what was implicit in Piaget's schema, and the third stage stresses the external and internal aspects of self-accepted moral principles.

Neither Piaget nor Freud has a positive theory which de-   **2.***8* scribes the conditions under which rational morality develops, except Freud's suggestion of love relationships in early years, and Piaget has been described as having merely shown that the distinction between customary and rational morality actually has application (26). Piaget was the first to admit that

'it is also conceivable that intelligence alone might suffice to sharpen the child's evaluation of conduct without necessarily inclining him to do good actions.'

Studies over a long period have in fact revealed that there is often very little tangible connection between the moral judgments and the moral nature of children (5) (12). In a large study of 10,000 American school children Hartshorne and May were concerned with their moral behaviour, as distinct from their moral judgments. They could not make a division between the very honest and the very dishonest since most of the standards of honesty were specific to given situations (15).

There is always a gap between what a child knows is right and what he would do in a given situation. Thus in Hartshorne and May's study there was a substantial but not large correlation between types of honesty and a test of moral knowledge. This tendency was recently noticed by Morris (23), and with it there was a slow decline with age in judgments founded on self-interest, particularly in the area of what would actually be done.

Heredity and Environment

2.9   The link between what should be done and what would be done is, in a sense, the conscience or super-ego, which is developed by conditioning and learning in the social environment (27). It is interesting to recall that there is no word in ancient Greek or medieval Latin which adequately conveys the meaning of our present word "conscience", and we have to conclude that the concept is a cultural one. A child's concept of wrong is what society has taught him is wrong, and an important factor in this is the socio-economic level of the family from which he comes. A study by Harrower (14) of children of 6 to 11 years of age who were presented with the problem of cheating and copying illustrates this: those from the relatively high socio-economic group tended to say that it does no good to cheat or copy, or that it is not the way to study, while those from lower groups usually spoke of it as unfair, lying, and forbidden. The authoritarian influence in the lower groups was accompanied by their acceptance of the need for more severe punishment than that anticipated by higher groups. There is also a tendency for higher groups to arrive more quickly at consistency in their values. The environmental factor is important since, as Harrower says,

> 'the very fact that a child will imbibe some parts of his intellectual atmosphere and not others, and again, that children must inevitably grow up in different atmospheres and be subject to different influences is of great importance in the study of development.'

Heredity reinforces environment since high intelligence in **2.***10* parents usually leads to high intelligence in children, and the result is a degree of economic security obtained through well-paid jobs and an atmosphere in which the temptations to hold views of low morality are minimised. The danger of such families is that there may be correspondingly less emotional security where children feel that economic and material comfort have been made a substitute for love and understanding. Parental indifference is easily confused with the smaller degree of parental constraint which intelligent and affluent parents often exercise. There are few subjects on which there is more unwarranted generalisation than on the question of parental influence on moral values, and the most frequently asserted opinion is that there is a constant decline in dependence on parents. In fact, there may be an increase in dependence at various stages, and this will vary not only from one family to another but from one area of moral values to another. The major difference may be that high status parents may help their children more quickly towards cognitive moral maturity and low status parents more quickly towards emotional moral maturity.

The environmental factors which Havighurst and Taba **2.***11* reported as strongly conditioning the beliefs of adolescents were families, community **mores** or standards, religion, and the influence of their fellows. Clear relationships have been detected between various kinds of aggressive or inhibited behaviour among children and the kinds of home from which they come (16). In this situation the line between heredity and environment is difficult to draw, though experiments with bringing up identical twins in different families have pointed strongly to the influence of environment. There is little doubt that the home is the fundamental influence, but given other favourable influences, there is a possibility that some of the bad influence of homes can be overcome. Sociometric studies have revealed that the group can be a powerful influence for good or evil in attitude modification (9). The **mores** of the society of which the group is only a part may or may not be in harmony with the aims of the group.

Mass Media

2.*12*   Mass media, which reflect changes in public taste and standards and possibly influence them further, present difficulties to the researcher. Research on their influence is partly speculative, and because of changes in the nature of the media it tends to get out of date quickly. It is obviously important to consider the effects of the exposure of the child to the influence of mass media. Radio, as a medium, has been regarded as lacking impact, partly because of its lack of visual stimulation. Children's devotion to radio is largely confined to listening to pop music, and the recent attention to social problems in the lyrics of this music, at whatever level of intellect, may be regarded as showing concern.

2.*13*   The visual stimulation which is obtainable from the cinema and television may be said to create a different situation. The usual answer to criticisms concerning the allegedly bad moral influence which cinema and television are said to exert has been that they act as a form of catharsis, and that the effects are neither as bad nor as good as people suggest. The fact that it lacks lasting influence suggests that the question of the relation of the media to reality, and the application which values offered by mass media have to real life may be seen to be limited (17). Television, in particular, may broaden interests. It encourages new sports, stimulates reading of dramatised novels, and brings the individual into direct and immediate contact with the greatest social and international problems.

There seems little evidence that television has provided an **2.***14* alternative to youth clubs among adolescents. While membership of youth clubs is not as high as many would hope, for those who do attend there are many opportunities for cooperation on a practical level. More important perhaps than the total membership of clubs is the fact that those children who need such facilities most— those from poorer homes—seem on average to attend less than children from more affluent backgrounds (10). Wealth is an inadequate measure of the moral tone of a family, but the proven connection between poverty and delinquency makes the provision of facilities for poorer classes most urgent.

Similar interpretations have been made concerning the influence of the cinema. It has been assumed that moral laxity, hooliganism and mischievous behaviour could not be directly attributed to films, and that the presentation of false standards— strength, luck, beauty and money—only precipitate actions in those already inclined to do them (29).

If the results of recent research are confirmed, there may be **2.***15* wisdom in suspecting that mass media have a larger effect than is sometimes supposed. Children, when asked for their ideal person or hero, have shown that over the years mass media personalities replaced religious, historical and family personalities.

In a study of children's ideal persons drawn from mass media Benaim (3) has shown the choices of boys and girls and the number making the choices, as the following table reveals:

Boys		**Girls**	
Choice	*No. making the choice*	*Choice*	*No. making the choice*
The Saint	14	Cilla Black	11
Churchill	11	Sandie Shaw	10
James Bond	9	Kathy Kirby	8
Danger Man	5	Dusty Springfield	6
Cliff Richard	5	Twinkle	6
Captain Burke	4	Mary Poppins	6
Charlie Chaplin	4	Elizabeth Taylor	4
Mick Jagger	3	Hayley Mills	4
John Lennon	3	Margot Fonteyn	3
Ringo Starr	3	Dr Who	3
George Bostham	3	Barbara (from Dr Who)	3
Shakespeare	2	Vicky (from Dr Who)	2
Dr Who	2	James Bond	2
The Lone Ranger	2	Honor Blackman	2
Paul McCartney	2	The Saint	2
Arthur Ransome	2	Diana Dors	2
Tom Sawyer	2	Julie Andrews	2
Danny Kaye	2	Betsy (in The Five Find-Outers)	2

Benaim's study showed that almost no child aged between 7 and 11 selected a religious person, Joan of Arc, not in the above table, being one of the few such persons chosen. In the past Christ was chosen frequently, but it was his ability to work miracles rather than his divinity that aroused admiration. This is one reason for not being too alarmed at the replacement of Christ by "The Saint" of the television series, for the choice in each case is based on the ability of the chosen hero to show personal prowess, and it may be hoped that this juvenile approach will disappear.

In the same study the gradual drop in the number of children who chose a parent as an ideal may be healthy if it reflects a more realistic relationship with parents. The tendency of many mass media is to confuse fiction and reality, and thus do no more than recognise juvenile feelings in us all. What is necessary is the ability to keep the line between fiction and reality as clear as possible, and to encourage the recognition of the good qualities of those whom one lives and works with, and of those who have actually lived in the world.

The School

It is less important that the school should self-consciously **2.***16* enforce Christian ideals of conduct than that, influenced by Christian goals, the school should be seen by all its members as one in which respect and affection between teacher and child should be given maximum scope. The effects of a definite religious training on morals are difficult to measure, and research findings are inconclusive. The capacity, however, for giving and receiving affection influences the way in which the child responds to the moral teaching of his elders. Pupils react differently to different teachers, and this affects the way in which they come to like a subject and the credence which may be given to the values the teacher is seen to hold (30). The social cohesion and interaction between pupils, and between teacher and pupils, is greater in classes with a 'good' climate (6). Since the child learns his concept of self from comments made by others and inferences from his own experiences, modification is possible in the self-picture (28).

In the classroom there is always a conflict between two oppos- **2.***17* ing tendencies: the dominative situation where the child satisfies his needs without regard to others, and the integrative situation where ways are found of reaching those goals which are satisfying to him and his fellows, thus establishing conditions for cooperative enterprise (1).

Frequently in group work a leader of activities emerges, and research findings on this subject have a bearing on the work of the teacher. In an authoritarian situation the leader remains aloof, preventing open, though not latent, aggression. The opposite position, one of *laissez-faire*, leaves too much to individuals and leads to frustration and bad behaviour. The best situation is where the alternatives are discussed, the children forming their own groups, from which a leadership develops which is not so strongly imposed that it stultifies initiative and cooperation.

Summary

2.1**–2.**8

Moral maturity, whether one talks about moral knowledge or moral behaviour, is difficult to define. This is a major reason for the difficulty of measurement, since Piaget's discussion has been in terms of development through stages, rather than precise definitions of moral maturity as such. The child begins by accepting the rules imposed by authority and ends by seeing that the rules have to be interpreted in the particular situation and with reference to the motives underlying the thought or action. Kohlberg's revision of this scheme suggests there is more than one type of moral attitude at any stage, and that we must remember that the early stages of development are really pre-moral. There is often little connection between the measured moral knowledge and observed moral behaviour or measured moral judgments of a person.

2.9**–2.**11

It is likely that children from lower socio-economic families interpret moral behaviour more in terms of the rules, and punishment for infringing them, than those from higher levels. In addition, higher status parents tend to encourage their children to reach earlier cognitive moral maturity, and lower status parents encourage earlier emotional moral maturity.

2.*12*–**2.***15*

The effect on moral values of mass media is generally believed to be small, and to some extent the effect rests on the separation which is made between fantasy and reality. Mass media inform the child about moral issues, even to the extent of influencing him to demonstrate his feelings on war, racial discrimination and other problems. It is often claimed that mass media only influence for evil those who are already predisposed to it. The choice of admired persons from such sources may be for reasons just as juvenile as those which account for the high number of historical and religious persons chosen in the past.

2.*16*–**2.***17*

The School should encourage respect and affection between children and teacher. In this situation the teacher can influence the moral and intellectual development of the child more effectively, and ways can be found for each individual to reach his goals without frustrating the attempts of others. Natural leadership among children should be allowed to develop, and the teacher can assert an occasional but firm intervention in the activities of the class.

Questions for Discussion

1. What help have teachers been given by research into moral education?
2. In the light of research how ought teaching to take account of class differences?
3. In what ways do mass media debase values?
4. Are we born with the capacity to distinguish good and evil?
5. Make a list, individually or collectively, of 10 moral evils. Rank them in order of importance and justify your choices.

Bibliography

(1)

Anderson, H. H. **Domination and Integration in the Social Behaviour of Young Children in an Experimental Play situation.** *Genet. Psychol. Monogr., 19, 341–408, 1937.*

(2)

Beller, E. K. **Two Attitude Components in Younger Boys.** *J. Soc. Psychol., 29, 137–151, 1949.*

(3)

Benaim, S. *Summary of a lecture to an* **I.T.A. Conference 1965.** *The Observer, January 21, 1968.*

(4)

Bloom, L. **A Reappraisal of Piaget's Theory of Moral Judgment.** *J. of Genet. Psychol., 95, 3–12, 1959.*

(5)

Chassels, C. F.
Chassels, E. B.
Chassels, L. M.
A Test of Ability to Weigh Foreseen Consequences. *Teachers' College Record, 25, 39–50, 1924.*

(6)

Connor, D. V. **Behaviour in Class Groups of Contrasting Climate.** *Brit. J. Educ. Psychol., 30, 244–249, 1960.*

(7)

Descoeudres, A. **Sur le Jugement Moral.** *L'Intermediaire des Educateurs, 2, 54, 1914.*

(8)
Edwards, J. B. **Some Moral Attitudes of Boys in a Secondary Modern School.**
Educ. Rev., 1⁷, 114–28, 1965.

(9)
Evans, K. M. **Sociometry and Education.**
London: Routledge and Kegan Paul, 1962.

(10)
Evans, K. M. **Club Members Today.**
London: National Association of Mixed Clubs and Girls' Clubs, 1960.

(11)
Gesell, A. **Youth: the Years from 10 to 16.**
London: Hamish Hamilton, 1956.

(12)
Haines, T. H. **Diagnostic Values of Some Performance Tests.**
Psychol. Rev., 22, 299–305, 1915.

(13)
Harding, D. W. **Social Psychology and Individual Values.**
London: Hutchinson, 1953.

(14)
Harrower, M. R. **Social Status and the Moral Development of the Child.**
Brit. J. Educ. Psychol., 4, 75–95, 1934.

(15)
Hartshorne, H. **Studies in Deceit.**
May, M. A. *New York: Macmillan, 1928.*

(16)

Hewitt, L. E. **Fundamental Patterns of Maladjust-**
Jenkins, R. L. **ment—The Dynamics of their Origin.**
Illinois: Green, 1946.

(17)

Himmelweit, H. T. **Television and the Child.**
Oppenheim, A. N. *Oxford University Press, 1958.*
Vince, P.

(18)

Isaacs, S. *Review of J. Piaget's* **Moral Judgement**
of the Child.
Mind, 43, 85–99, 1934.

(19)

Kohlberg, L. **Moral development and identification.**
Child Psychology. 62nd Yearbook of the
National Society for the Study of Education.
Part I, 227–332. Chicago: University of
Chicago Press, 1964.

(20)

Lerner, E. **Constraint Areas and the Moral**
Judgment of Children.
Menasha, Wisconsin, 1937.

(21)

Macaulay, E. **An Investigation into the Moral**
Watkins, S. H. **Development of the Moral Concep-**
tions of Children.
Forum of Education, 4, 13–33, 1926.

(22)

Macrae, D. **A Test of Piaget's Theories of Moral**
Development.
J. Abnorm. Soc. Psychol., 49, 14–18, 1954.

(23)
Morris, J. F. **The Development of Adolescent Value-Judgments.**
Brit. J. Educ. Psychol., 28, 1–14, 1958.

(24)
Peters, R. S. **Freud's Theory of Moral Development in Relation to that of Piaget.**
Brit. J. Educ. Psychol., 30, 250–58, 1960.

(25)
Piaget, J. **The Moral Judgement of the Child.**
London: Routledge and Kegan Paul, 1932.

(26)
Peel, E. A. **Experimental Examination of some of Piaget's Schemata.**
Brit. J. Educ. Psychol., 29, 89–103, 1959.

(27)
Sherif, M. **An Outline of Social Psychology.**
New York: Harper, 1948.

(28)
Staines, J. W. **The Self-Picture as a Factor in the Classroom.**
Brit. J. Educ. Psychol. 18, 97–111, 1958.

(29)
Wheare Report **Report of the Department Committee on Children and the Cinema.**
H.M.S.O., 1950.

(30)
Wilson, J. **Introduction to Moral Education.**
Williams, N. *Penguin Books, 1968.*
Sugarman, B.

3 Moral Values and Children

The Primary School Child

Moral development is closely associated with emotional and social development. The child forms his sense of personal worth and his moral sense from early experiences of acceptance, approval, and disapproval. Out of an externally imposed rule of what is permitted arises a sense of what ought to be done and an internal system of control: in everyday terms, a conscience. The very young child, limited in understanding, acts according to strict rules, even though he breaks them. What is right and wrong relates closely to what his parents say and to situations arising in the home. Later, as the child develops intellectually and lives with others, his sense of right and wrong derives from a wider circle and becomes more qualified; the rules of a game are seen to be arrived at by a consensus, and therefore modifiable by common agreement. Even so, the 11 year old still has a fairly crude and concrete sense of justice. It appears doubtful whether an autonomous conscience is established before adolescence. **Plowden Report Children and their Primary Schools** *Vol. 1, p. 25.*

It is in the primary school that the child develops for the **3.1**
first time a measurement of the ethical sense, learning how to
adjust to a wider variety of persons and situations than he has
hitherto encountered. Here he evolves a sense of 'mine and thine',
'right and wrong', and 'good and bad'. He learns to handle his
aggression, share, show consideration, and assume small amounts
of responsibility in the everyday activities of the school. (6) Pro-
ceeding on the principle of starting from the known, he learns to
get on with others before he can develop an abstract conception
of what is required when he meets other people. For most of the
time, the child's idea of wrong is determined for him by parent or
teacher, the break with conventional morality not coming before
he has left the primary school. This does not make the understanding of the moral values of the primary school child much
easier for, just as Goldman (8) has shown that in the minds of the
infant and the very young religion and life are inseparable, so are
the problems of morality and life. If one is to appreciate fully
the minds of this age-group their views of morality cannot be seen
in isolation, since it is in the nature of the child that he cannot
discuss morality as a separate phenomenon. Children do not consciously engage in moral discussion in the primary school, and
the most fruitful pursuit for those who would understand these
children is, therefore, to follow—in works like those of Gabriel (5)
and Madge (13)—the thoughts of children in their search for
meaning in the process of growing up.

When he enters the infant school the child's concept of **3.2**
good is almost entirely egocentric and hedonistic; values are
formed with reference to the effect they have on the self, and
operate on a pleasure pain principle. This is most obvious in the
infant's choice of certain food as 'good', but in the case of the
importance attached to helping parents or saying one's prayers,
the explanation is rather more indirect. The former evokes praise,
and the latter gives feelings of security to supplement that given

by parents. Because the infant is not yet in a position to menace society, and has in fact to be protected, the things he considers bad are those things he has been taught to avoid for his own safety —fighting, dirtiness, and playing in the road. He may come near to externalising a sense of 'bad' by describing as such the action of a kitten in running away, but the main reason is likely to be the unpleasant effects the action of the kitten has on the child by endangering the attachment which the child has formed and the pleasure he derives from the attachment.

3.3   By the time he comes to leave the infant school two very important developments have usually taken place: he has some idea of the value of helping others and makes the conventional response in realising the evil of major social problems like stealing. The recognition of stealing as bad is curious in view of the decreased importance to the child at this stage of personal possessions, and leads one to suppose that condemnation of stealing bears no relation to the child's ability to understand the feelings of the person robbed, but is instead a view adopted under adult pressure. In contrast, helping others is a more positive activity, which can be experienced at this age either in the school or in small projects outside the school, aimed at helping the old or sick.

3.4   The resulting growth of the awareness of self, as opposed to the attention paid to the gratification of the child's own senses, is linked to the need for praise. Responsiveness to praise tends to become greater than that to physical punishment. Linked with intellectual development is an increased facility for the use of reason by older infants, and the more lucid verbalisation of experience. This leads the hearer to suppose a greater independence and maturity than is actually the case. The older infant values highly his growing independence, such as crossing the road on his own, or writing with the minimum of help, but his ability to verbalise these experiences does not involve an equal ability to generalise from these rudimentary experiences. When told of

Florence Nightingale's work in the Crimea, for example, the child will view it all in his own terms. The way in which so many see her actions as disobedience, involving hunger, loneliness and exposure to cold weather, shows that they do not appreciate the qualities of adulthood, and can only interpret the story in terms of the consequences if a child himself should be in that position.

Throughout the junior school the child increases his ability **3.5** to generalise, and the most likely values are those of fairness and honesty, which can be so strict as to appear to older people to be self-righteous. Madge (13) has shown the interest which juniors have in religious matters, involving as they do the natural curiosity, doubts and bewilderment of all human intellectual activity, and at least a concern for moral issues, if not yet a facility to generalise about them with much success. The obligation not to tell tales or to lie is the beginning of a feeling of personal responsibility, but at this stage bears little relation to the seriousness of the promise or the possibility of other general considerations which might make breaking the promise a more honourable course.

In the last year or two of the junior school the major values **3.6** appear, so that it is recognised to be wrong to kill, rob or intimidate, and these are seen to have general application. The need to tell white lies is occasionally recognised to be necessary in order to avoid hurting other people's feelings (1). Of major significance is the inability, even at this stage, to sustain for long the general impression that values of varying degrees of importance should be recognised as such. Among the more significant values are those attached to bravery, loyalty, truthfulness and kindness, but the importance ascribed to them is frequently indistinguishable from values associated with the removal of cheeky or boastful behaviour. The inference is that the oldest junior school child still finds it difficult to differentiate the values which are necessary for the maintenance of good relations within his own group, and those which are of greater importance in society at large. (16)

3.7   A major interest of the junior school is the way in which norms are established firstly from interactions between the teacher's intentions and the outlook of the majority of the pupils, and later from the values projected by the more prominent girls' and boys' groups within the class (4). In fact a group's values may come to be most clearly expressed by its 'leading crowd'. This is frequently the outcome of value-systems emerging from the considerable social mixing which arises from a school's catchment area. The more numerous and vigorous tend to predominate, especially if they are middle-class in origin—a fact which is important in the choice of whether or not to stream.

3.8   In terms of misdeeds and punishment the development of the child's thought may be summarised as follows (2): having been told the story of a child's misdeeds, children from 6 until 8 years of age usually cling to a traditional view that punishment is morally necessary as expiation and deterrent. Thereafter, children gradually see retribution, the inflicting of 'equal' suffering, as ineffective in modifying behaviour, and justifiable only as a measure

'to make the offender realise in what way he has broken the bond of solidarity.'

The attempt to put oneself in another's place, the law of reciprocity, tends towards a morality of forgiveness and understanding.

The Secondary School Child

'Education can only function within the broad directives of right and wrong which society gives. Teachers and youth leaders are, however, well placed to bring to attention the personal bewilderment and disaster to which this public indecision over moral issues often leads the young . . .. It seems to us quite possible to imagine a society in which teenagers had their present freedom to live their own lives; but in which they were not deprived of the security which comes from a well understood knowledge of what is right and what is wrong. After all, it was the adults and not the teenagers who first cast doubt on the rules.' **Crowther Report. 15 to 18,** *Vol. 2, p. 38.*

3.9 Recognising that the immutable laws of earlier childhood no longer apply, the adolescent builds his own moral code. (7) It is often only when the pupil is over half way through the secondary course that a real break with conventional morality occurs. He is often, therefore, about 14 years old before he realises that morality and moral values really demand a personal decision, and that while a value may have considerable logical and emotional appeal, it is often necessary in practice to take action which departs from the principle. Swainson (18) concluded that hardly a boy or girl over 10 years was encountered who did not have a high standard of moral knowledge. This reminds us of the conclusions of Redl and Wineman (17) who, having looked at many problem children, never saw a child who had no conscience at all. In the realms of practical action, values based on pure self-interest tend to disappear, and, despite fluctuations around puberty, there is also an increasing independence of judgment. This growing personal confidence allows for generosity of spirit, and the assumption that what the adolescent wants for himself should also be allowed to others. There is adequate evidence, however, that more intelligent pupils have more complex values, illustrating the contention that the pressures towards conformity are greater among the less intelligent (15).

3.10 Most adolescents still live with their parents and although some deference to parental values has to be shown, there are areas where conflicts of values are traditionally strong. Obviously the conflicts are most likely to be greatest on questions of personal freedom, sex and religion. The importance of personal freedom to come and go, wear what one likes, and such matters, has always been subordinated in popular discussion to problems of sexual morality. This latter problem has the most immediate relevance for the adolescent, and social change has made them more critically relevant. More adolescents go away to college, have holidays in mixed company and possess an earning power unknown to previous generations.

3.11   The amount of conflict that exists between the generations frequently arises out of the actions to be taken on a set of values, and not from the values themselves. A parent may therefore share with his adolescent son or daughter the view that killing or violence is wrong, but find it hard to condone his son's sharing in violent demonstrations against war. Like their elders, adolescents have values connected with the trivial as well as the important, but when pressed it is customary for them to admit that some matters—war and peace, social inequality, sexual ethics and racial discrimination, for example, raise issues of greater weight than, say, sport or pop music.

3.12   The adolescent 'ideal' differs from that of the primary school child, for the latter's view of reality confines his choice to parents and relatives whom he actually knows, whereas the wider education and intellectual consciousness of the adolescent allows him to choose historical, fictional, sporting and film-star personalities. What surprises many observers is the tendency of adolescents to stress conventional moral proprieties (like honesty and politeness) rather more than kindness and generosity (14). Taba (18) has shown that they tend to accept the familiar cultural stereotypes without enquiring into their relevance for themselves. It would not be surprising if the abler children in secondary schools showed a higher level of moral concept in view of correlations detected between the level of moral concept and the level of logical reasoning (8) (11). Personality ratings by means of I.P.A.T. tests also show that subjects having a 'good personality' make higher moral judgments (12).

Although the more pessimistic prophecies concern the future **3.***13* of adolescent moral values, it is difficult, partly because of conceptual difficulties, to say whether the expression of moral proprieties is specifically Christian. However, the table below suggests that we must be particularly cautious before assenting to the view that there has been a great shift among adolescents in their recognition of moral evils. The table shows the views of youth over the years on the relative seriousness of various social evils (10):

1919	*Rank*	**1954**
killing, murder	1	killing, murder
sexual misbehaviour	2	use or sale of narcotics
stealing	3	sexual misbehaviour
cheating	4	stealing
lying	5	drinking (alcohol)
drinking (alcohol)	6	cheating
gambling	7	lying
swearing, vulgar talk	8	being cruel
not being religious	9	not being religious
being selfish	10	reckless driving
gossiping	11	swearing
idleness	12	being undependable
snobbishness	13	gossiping
extravagance	14	being inconsiderate
smoking	15	smoking
dancing	16	being conceited

As these views were those of American youth, caution has to be exercised in assuming their relevance in all countries, but in English-speaking countries, especially, some attention should be directed to them. On major questions there is no conflict over 35 years, and the major interest lies in the way the views reveal a change in social life and attitudes. The appearance of drugs as a social problem in 1954 reminds us of the still more urgent problem now. By 1954 reckless driving was considered deplorable, but in view of its danger at the present time, as revealed in accident figures and official reaction in advertising and legislation, one may suppose that this may well be more recognised now than ever. The views of 1954 show the move away from the worst aspects of puritanism—for example dancing, an evil in 1919, was no mentioned in 1954. The major change of emphasis in which one can take comfort is the greater awareness of the need for good personal relationships, especially the need to be dependable and considerate.

3.14   The more optimistic outlook is encouraged by a study of the work of Eppel and Eppel (3). Their investigation of the 'focal concerns' of some 250 working class, day-release students of 15–18 years is not claimed to be representative of all adolescents, but the sample selected is of greater interest because they are no longer subject to the moral influence of school. Schools have already exerted whatever influence they possessed, and we are thus looking at the effects of parental and school influence, and the values evolved by membership of their group at work.

3.15   The tendency on all sides to think of adolescence as a separate stage of development makes communication between the generations more difficult. This has led adolescents to think of themselves as

> 'belonging to a generation handicapped by distorted stereotypes about their behaviour and moral standards' (3).

Evidence of this poor communication is adult denunciation, not always justly founded, of adolescent immorality, but apologists of the 'new morality' may, as Eppel and Eppel say, create a new stereotype which may not correspond well with the rather more conventional picture adolescents themselves present.

Eppel and Eppel found that only a minority had a generalised hostility to authority. Most wish to discuss rationally the sources of authority, and value honesty, loyalty, family life and marriage. What matters more to them than traditional sanctions is

'the quality of personal relationships'

which is

'the touchstone for their assessment of their own and other people's moral standards.'

Summary

3.*1***–3.***8*

In the primary school the child learns the rudimentary sense of 'right and wrong', his thinking on this being inseparable from his whole thought process and his shared experiences with others. Gradually values based on self-interest disappear, some awareness of the feelings of others is acquired, and a recognition is shown of the existence of major evils. The ability to generalise on social and moral problems remains undeveloped in the top classes of the junior school. A major contribution to moral values is played by the group, and punishment becomes justifiable in that its power shows how the offender has broken the bond of solidarity.

3.*9***–3.***15*

The adolescent moral code is to some extent a reconstruction and modification of his earlier code. This involves more personal decisions, an awareness of the gap between moral knowledge and moral judgment, and a greater tolerance, especially among the more intelligent, when a person fails to bridge the gap. The significance attached to the moral values of adolescents varies, and on important issues the adolescent is more likely than the adult to have an optimistic view of the efficiency of acting to remedy a wrong. Adolescent ideals are taken from a wider area of experience than that possessed by younger children. Studies of adolescent moral knowledge and concerns suggest that the more alarmist talk of a decline in adolescent morality in the widest sense may be partly unfounded.

Questions for Discussion

1. From your experience of younger children, how far can you go towards acquiring a knowledge of their values?

2. How may the two concepts of authority and participation be best balanced and applied in school, bearing in mind the values of children at different ages?

3. In terms of development, how do adolescent values represent an advance on those of pre-adolescence?

4. Are adult remarks about adolescent immorality clear, and are they justified?

5. What are the implications for the training of teachers of the values described in this chapter?

Bibliography

(1)
Bradburn, E. **Children's Moral Knowledge.**
Educational Research, 9, 203–7, 1967.

(2)
Brearley, M. **A Teacher's Guide to Reading Piaget.**
Hitchfield, E. *London: Routledge and Kegan Paul, 1966.*

(3)
Eppel, E. M. **Adolescents and Morality.**
Eppel, M. *London: Routledge and Kegan Paul, 1966.*

(4)
Evans, K. M. **Sociometry and Education.**
London: Routledge and Kegan Paul, 1962.

(5)
Gabriel, J. **Children Growing up.**
London: University of London Press, 1964.

(6)
Gesell, A. **The Child From Five to Ten.**
London: Hamish Hamilton, 1946.

(7)
Gesell, A. **Youth—The Years from Ten to**
Ilg, F. L. **Sixteen.**
Ames, L. R. *London: Hamish Hamilton, 1956.*

(8)
Goldman, R. J. **Religious Thinking from Childhood
to Adolescence.**
London: Routledge and Kegan Paul, 1964.

(9)
Goldman, R. J. **Readiness for Religion: a basis for developmental religious education.** *London: Routledge and Kegan Paul, 1965.*

(10)
Horton, R. E. **Some Ethical Values of Youth,**
Remmers, H. H. **Compared over the Years.** *Report No. 38 Purdue Opinion Panel, Vol. 13, 2, 1–3, 1954.*

(11)
Kohlberg, L. **Children's Orientation towards a Moral Order.** *Vita Humana, 6, 11–33, 1963.*

(12)
Longhran, R. **A Pattern of Development in Moral Judgment made by Adolescents Derived from Piaget's Schema of the Development in Childhood.** *Educational Review, 19, 79–98, 1967.*

(13)
Madge, V. **Children in Search of Meaning.** *London: S.C.M. Press, 1965.*

(14)
Mitchell, C. **Do Virtues and Vices Change?** *School and Society, 57, 111–12, 1943.*

(15)
Morris, J. F. **The Development of Adolescent Moral Judgments.** *Brit. J. Educ. Psychol., 28, 1–14, 1958.*

(16)

Pringle, M. L. K. **Some Moral Concepts and Judgments**
Edwards, J. B. **of Junior School Children.**
Brit. J. Soc. Clin. Psychol. (In press),
1965.

(17)

Redl, F. **The Aggressive Child.**
Wineman, D. *Glencoe Free Press, 1957.*

(18)

Swainson, B. M. **The Development of Moral Ideas in**
Children and Adolescents.
Ph.D. thesis. University of Oxford, 1949.

(19)

Taba, H. **The Moral Beliefs of 16 Year Olds**
in The Adolescent: A Book of Readings, ed.
J. Seidman. New York: Dryden Press, 1953.

4 The Teacher and the School

The Role of the Teacher

4._1_ In view of our discussion of the philosophical and psychological difficulties surrounding the teaching of moral values, and the transmission of values through one's peers in an informal way, the task before the teacher who wishes to play a significant part in this aspect of the personal development of children would appear to be daunting. To begin with, the teacher has to recognise that he is not the individual with the most powerful moral influence: generally that position is occupied by the parents, who consciously or unconsciously transmit moral values in a way which makes them the most potent moral tutors of the young (3) (4) (23). This not only reminds the teacher of the limits of his influence but also of the need to avoid setting up situations where conflict is likely to arise between the values of the parents and those of the teacher or school. Many an earnest teacher has discovered, with considerable dismay, that an attitude of the child which he considers undesirable is endorsed or viewed with indifference by parents—a situation which is most common when the teacher educates children of a class dissimilar from that in which his own origins lie.

4._2_ The respective roles of parent and teacher are fairly clearly defined. The parent is the major source of values, possessing sanctions, such as the withdrawal of pocket-money, deprivation of privileges or parental consent, which are more compelling than those available to the school. The teacher, although in a more authoritative role, possesses fewer sanctions and yet has to provide for the acquisition of moral values in a framework much larger than the family. The school brings the child into contact with competitive work—and play—situations and it is very largely from his peers that the child acquires his values. The teacher is often said to act *in loco parentis*, which logically requires that he should teach those values which parents teach. Teachers cannot normally know what the parents individually require and cannot differentiate between the requirements in the case of each individual child, even if they could bring themselves to teach conflicting values. One function of the teacher that has increased is the need to counteract the tendency of the highly rational yet permissive parent who gives no guidance. Wilson (24) has described the teacher's authority over the child as a mandate rather than absolute moral rights. We may wish to make children more rational in forming their own values, and produce neither conformity nor rebellion, but unless the teacher believes in the superiority of the values he has worked out for himself, it may be doubted whether he will make a great contribution in his professional work.

In practice, however, the teacher makes his own contribution, whether or not he is aware of the problems. The greatest success is often achieved by those with the least awareness of the intellectual difficulties surrounding moral education, but possessing personal qualities which more than outweigh their lack of awareness. This reminds us that moral education can be achieved by those who live out morality rather than think about it. This applies equally to teacher and child, so that there is a lack of self-consciousness in both. In the child it is likely to be largely a question of acceptance, and in the adult, a recognition, however poorly analysed, of the limits of reason. A superficial kind of success has also been achieved by those who, arguing that children

4.3

cannot be allowed the freedom to develop in a way which might be unacceptable to their elders, have imposed on them values which are considered desirable by adult authority. The depth of conviction of these values, and their consequent length of life, are open to question, since they are based neither on the child's interests as seen by him, nor on any subsequent authority which will maintain them when he leaves the sphere of influence of the teacher. It is worth recalling that, while in most matters the teacher is considered to be a person with radical convictions, (for example in politics), in the question of morality, as the agent for transmitting traditional values concerning the moral role of the individual in society, his position has been a more conservative one.

4.4   Those who deny the practicability of **teaching moral values** have a case. A value is something accepted as reasonable and necessary; it is 'caught rather than taught', and can be given up later when it is considered no longer relevant. The weakness of the argument lies in its mistaken view of the nature and aims of modern teaching, by which the didactic character of teaching is well on the way to being replaced by a situation where teacher and child explore individual experience and external phenomena together. This allows problems to be made objective and the subject of discussion, rather than the formal teaching of ready-made solutions to various moral dilemmas. Just as factual knowledge in mathematics is graded according to the age and ability of the pupil, so the approach to the moral issue must also take account of these factors.

4.5   In moral education age matters more than intelligence or even social background. The phrase 'the generation gap' may be new, but Plato in the Eighth Book of **The Republic** commented,

'Teachers are afraid of their pupils and pander to them,
    and pupils despise their teachers.'

If anything akin to this regrettable circumstance arises, it is almost certain to involve a conflict over a moral problem; and the conflict will arise, not simply from the teacher—pupil relationship as such, but from the age difference. The teacher's ability to inform the child on skills will usually go unchallenged, but the relevance of anything he says on moral questions will often be questioned, because it is assumed that the position of authority, and especially the age of the teacher, makes his moral assumptions quite different from those of the children. Partly this may be due to the child's expectation of and perhaps need for a more authoritarian code against which it can give him some satisfaction to rebel.

4.6 There is no doubt that the desire to do good is a prime motive of those wishing to become teachers (22), and, as Evans (8) says, the teacher with a sense of mission is a person to be reckoned with, otherwise he would not be much use as a teacher of anything. There is evidence that the student-teacher realises the difficulties of his profession, and he is aware that salaries and social status are not as favourable as one might hope. In the role of moral guide it is useful to appear as an interesting and successful person and it is only to be expected that many children think of success in material terms. Another difficulty facing the teacher is that constant contact with immature minds encourages an authoritarian attitude in the teacher, and this attitude is dropped outside school only with difficulty. Unnatural attempts at authoritarianism in conditions which are not always demanding them prevent many teachers relaxing and exercising a more permissive control (17).

The wish to do good, even in difficult circumstances, can thus lead to a state of tension which the teacher can resolve in one of three ways (11). First, the intropunitive answer is for the teacher to punish himself, with the associated feelings of guilt and remorse. Second, by impunitive methods, repressing the frustrating situation. The teacher thus makes himself unhappy, and except for the obvious effect this could possibly have on children, they are not directly affected. Finally, the extra-punitive course, directing aggression to an external object or person. This has the associated emotions of anger and resentment, leading to very adverse effects on the class. All three solutions do not remove the impediment which prevents the teacher's being in a position to offer real guidance, and the only satisfactory remedy may be the removal of the person from the circumstances which give rise to the problem.

4.7   Even if the teacher can be said to be successful, his state of success is not necessarily permanent and demands constant decision in order to preserve momentum. A major decision is to assess his role as a bringer of values. A distinction has been made between the 'cultural missionary' and the 'cultural crusader' (10). As the former his role may be the zealous bringer of values into an environment of poverty, but as the latter he may be best employed stimulating values in an affluent, subtopian area. Whatever the environment, the teacher has to decide what kind of leadership he is going to offer. The choice, if wisely made, depends on the personality and abilities of the person concerned. He starts with the premise that his position involves authority or the principles of legitimacy, which he exercises of right, but he can break away from a dependence on legitimacy in two ways, according to his preferences. Firstly, he can offer charismatic leadership, which stresses the force of his personality; this encourages discipleship rather than blind obedience, and is most satisfactory when exercised where the pupils are of similar intellectual standing to the teacher. The major criticism of this kind of leadership is that the child's mind can be imprisoned and a system of propaganda instituted. Secondly, the teacher can break away from a full dependence on legitimacy, stressing interest rather than charisma. While this is less dominating, it follows interest rather than inspires it, which is only satisfactory on those occasions when children's interests are considered worthwhile.

Adolescent response to leadership is particularly good when **4.***8* the teacher is able to establish a friendly relationship and show he has wide interests (12). He is then seen to be a person who is anxious to treat his pupils as far as possible in an individual manner, and is assumed, because of his breadth of interests, to be the kind of person whose guidance might be worth seeking. The kind of person who can offer this is likely to be a confident teacher, and the more he can allow pupil-participation, the more learning, independent thought and constructive attitudes one can expect (9). The point about this kind of teaching which is often missed is that there is never any abdication of authority by the teacher, who at certain times steps forward to organise the activities and elicit the ideas of pupils, and at other times allows activity of a constructive kind to proceed without his intervention. There is a point, of course, when the absence of intervention puts the teacher's whole position in jeopardy, and the completely *laissez-faire* attitude results in the class soon becoming confused as to its intended activity (14).

The continuity of role is more assured where, as in the case **4.***9* of the primary school teacher, education of a child is in the hands of one person, and where concern is less for individual subjects than for the whole training of the individual. It is not easy to get agreement among a large number of independent-minded people on the kind of moral climate they wish to have in school, but unless a minimum agreement is reached there is little hope of securing the community which is essential for the nurturing of lasting moral ideals. The whole aim, one might argue, should be to make Kant's belief that every human being is an end in himself an integral part of teaching. This involves asking the question, "Am I using others as ends, or as means to my own satisfaction?"

The Role of the School

4.*10*   What are the goals which the school should attempt to
achieve in order that it may actively encourage the formation of
sound moral values? The following ten, unelaborated proposals
have been suggested by Wilson, Sugarman and Williams (24).
Here some attempt is made to speculate as to how these aims
might be achieved.

a. **A secure framework in group identity.**

      Identification is a key concept in religious and moral educa-
tion. A sense of personal identity is encouraged by membership
of a group, for the individual gets a sense of his personal identity
through the relationships he sustains with the other members of
the group. Schools are composed of many groups, the formation
of which—for different purposes—is both inevitable and desirable,
and while it is natural that authority should wish these groups to
reflect the wider aims of society or even of the school, there is some
danger in destroying, or attempting to destroy, those groups
which do not. Besides having the effect, quite frequently, of
strengthening the group, there is the added complication of losing
what relationship those in authority still have over their pupils,
to whom membership of the group is a factor of the greatest
importance in their lives.

      In order to change attitudes for what it believes to be the
better, authority has to learn how to identify groups with the
major aims of society, for it is as members rather than as individuals that the change of attitudes is most easily brought about.
For those who are 'isolates' there is always the danger of undesirable conduct, although it is a fact that their isolation may be due
to their possession of moral values of too demanding a nature for
the rest of their fellows. This is true of some of those from a very
dogmatic religious background; and it is worth remembering
that a balance has to be struck between dogmatic instruction and

social tolerance if the child is to feel happy in the many groups he may find himself wishing to join.

b. **The need for a personal identity, especially in terms of feeling confident, successful, useful, and wanted, particularly in the case of underprivileged children.** Since fear and inhibition are poor bases on which to erect moral values, emotional stability and confidence have to be established. The emotionally maladjusted frequently fail to take account of intentions in moral issues, and stress instead the possible consequences. A mature judgment, resting as it does on a knowledge of the motives of the person involved, demands a high degree of stability. Confidence is essential in order to enter into relationships, have reasonable expectations of others, fulfil your obligations to them, and to survive those occasions when you or they fail to live up to certain standards which you had come to expect. Emotional stability can be encouraged by drama, games and a liberal atmosphere, the last being most important, so that the imposition of the former activities on the unwilling does not create more difficulties than they were intended to remedy. The person most requiring help, however, is the one whom the teacher does not automatically encourage, perhaps because of the low standard of his work or unpleasant traits of personality. Such a child soon sees no connection between his aspirations and those of the school, and there is a special need for strenuous efforts to discover some activity in which he can be involved. Traditionally this has been done by giving humdrum tasks, with lip-service being paid to its usefulness, but as Sybil Marshall has shown in **An Experiment in Education**, there is hardly anyone who has no talent at all. There is a stubborn insistence by most of us to classify one talent as superior to another, whereas, particularly in school, such distinctions are foolish and damaging to all concerned.

c. **Close personal contact with adults.**

The teacher is one of the adults with whom, in theory at

least, the child can develop a most fruitful relationship, and there are few who cannot recall the influence of a teacher in some part of their lives. Apart from the physical difficulty of establishing personal contacts in large classes, there is also the fear among many teachers of forming close relationships. Partly this is the authoritarian tradition, partly the fear that the greater intimacy might be abused by the child and lead to disciplinary trouble, and partly it is the wish to avoid the situation where contacts with some children become particularly close and lead to the charge of favouritism.

Despite these difficulties much can be done. From the experience of primary school teachers it is clear that once one abandons one's position of being constantly at the blackboard, and instead organises activities for the children to do individually or in groups, there is then freedom to mix with the children and offer guidance on matters not always related closely to the lesson. One of the great contributions of teachers of domestic subjects is precisely in the way they help their pupils investigate the moral bonds, especially of the family, which are essential for all to respect. The problem for all adults is to maintain the essence of maturity and authority which makes this advice worth more than advice gained from one's peers, without giving the impression of knowing the truth and wishing to impose it.

d. **The ability to develop moral concepts and communicate linguistically.**

Granted that there is a difference between 'doing morality' and 'thinking morality', there is still a level of moral concepts to which all must rise, and an ability to communicate one's moral ideas to others, which is essential to social life. The work of Piaget and others reminds us that there is no point in trying to develop in others moral concepts which are too difficult for them, but from about the age of seven years the process of discussing situations can begin. The issue has to be clarified if necessary, and the language made simple and direct. So often shallow verbalising of experience can lead to clichés, of which the common "I'm sorry" can be one of the most conspicuous. To avoid this the freer methods of language teaching can be used to explore the use of language as a means of expressing our feelings of moral obligation to others. What, we may ask, are the meanings to be attached to expressions of congratulations, sorrow, agreement and conflict? To what extent do certain situations and the language used bring out traditional responses, without feelings of a profound attachment to person or principle? An analysis of, and experimentation in the use of, language can therefore give the child an insight into the feelings of others, and a means of expressing in a rich and vibrant vocabulary what are his own true feelings (13). Bernstein (5) has argued that the use of categoric statements can, if frequently used, limit learning and curiosity and induce a sensitivity towards a

> 'particular type of authority in which social power is quickly and nakedly revealed.'

In the long run one may have to tell a child to "hold on tight" or "be quiet", but using a categoric statement too early prevents the child learning an area of connections and sequence and narrows the range of stimuli to which the child responds. Working-class language, Bernstein maintains, tends to be short, simple and repetitive. The implications of this theory are that progress in moral education depends on the acquisition by parents of a 'formal' language which allows a wider range of conceptual thought than the 'public' language which is characteristic of the working-class.

e. **Rule-governed activities.**

By now it is probably agreed that to describe morality in terms of rules is a gross simplification, and it may well be asked how participation in activities with rules to govern them can be said to aid moral development. Since Greek times the answer has been that, apart from their obvious physical value, activities such as games promote the psyche and harmonise the development of mind and body. This view received more recognition when Locke endorsed Juvenal's tag about

'the healthy mind in the healthy body'.

The implications for the individual in his relations seems to have come later, and it is doubtful whether the transfer of training is always sufficient to allow a good sportsman to apply his habits of cooperation and obeying the rules to all other aspects of his life.

Nevertheless sport does provide alternative value-systems: games provide opportunities for cooperation and are encouraged by the school, without being identified with its central purpose. They give a chance to learn the rudimentary sense of the inter-dependence of human beings and the need for written and unwritten rules in their activity. To some extent the life of the whole school has to be rule-governed, but, in order to work, the rules have to be seen to be relevant and necessary for all involved.

f. **The importance of parent-figures and of a firmly defined authority.**

In the day-school the role of the teacher *in loco parentis* is less obvious than in boarding schools, and providers of parent-figures or parent-substitutes must take account of this fact. Frequently even day-school teachers find themselves in the most demanding circumstances, in having to act as a substitute in the absence of a parent, or where parental authority is being inadequately exercised. The dangers of this are known to most teachers, and the relationship between parent and teacher in Britain is such that close consultation is very difficult. Contacts, when they occur, are usually in consciously contrived circumstances such as P.T.A. meetings or Open Days or Sports Days, which either make serious discussions difficult or emphasise too finely the respective roles of teacher and parent. Ideally the teacher should be in the position of being someone who is regarded as a person one can approach without his adopting an authoritative pose. Despite the natural reluctance of parents to enter schools which, although they are not aware of it at times, have become more liberal, the school can be used for their own activities and also be helped in its own aims and ventures. Ideally the teacher, if he has the time, should be able to visit the children's homes in a friendly way. In this way a realistic agreement on expectations could be established by him in consultation with parents.

g. **Channel aggression.**

It is too easy now to see aggression, as Freud saw it, as pathological,

> 'a deplorable impulse which ought to be eliminated, rather than a necessary part of our biological inheritance.'

As Storr (20) has shown, one face of aggression leads man to master his environment, attain independence, strive competitively, and attain successful male sexuality, while the other side is cruelty, torture, murder, war and madness. For Storr aggression becomes hostility and hatred when it contains an admixture of revenge. Among the causes are man's long, dependant infancy, the extremes of neglect or smothering love, which later affect behaviour through his unique memory and his tendency to react to present situations in terms of the past, (though this may be entirely unconscious) and his capacity for projection.

The vicious circle of aggression is that those most inclined to aggression are of low socio-economic status and when they experience the punishment which they expect, they become hardened to it and even more aggressive (7) (25)! How much, therefore, we can hope to change in the aggressive mentality is open to question. The conventional answers may work with some: sport, drama and movement, by consuming energy and giving a process of catharsis are a part of the remedy. The essentially ludicrous aspects of aggression can be brought out in dramatization which is

> 'at once the means by which the child ventures out into the characters and lives of others, and the means by which he draws back as symbols into the person of himself' (13).

h. **Cooperation not competition.**

Realism demands that we recognise that life is competitive and will remain so for the foreseeable future. It is, therefore, not in the child's interests to remove all competition from his work in school. In fact it is well known that most children like some competition, provided that opportunities are provided for all to experience success at something. Extremely competitive situations give rise to cheating, evasion and a distaste for learning and school life. The system of winning stars in primary schools or house points in secondary schools should, as a result, give credit not only to those who make academic or sporting progress, but also to those who show qualities of character. Group work at all levels, since it makes it possible for those with special gifts to help others, gives the giver and the receiver a point of contact centred in cooperation. At the same time, as Morris (17) points out, it is essential to arrange work to suit all levels if the children are not to feel cheated at the end of their school careers.

i. **Objectify feelings.**

The isolation of moral problems and their discussion as existing apart from the self enables the person to feel that others have the same problems and makes it possible to minimise feelings of guilt. In terms of the curriculum there is no more obvious place for this than in History where the actions of others can be objectively discussed without the pre-conceived ideas associated with religious studies. Apart from the difficulty of being objective, even about History, there are two problems (15). Firstly, there is the academic concern that History should not be concerned with moral issues, and secondly the more pressing problems that we must not exaggerate what the child can get out of social studies and stories of human relationships, for egocentricism is so great up to seven years that objectivity is very low (16). Piaget (18) describes how the terms 'brother' 'enemy' and 'foreigner' are absolute, not relative, to the child. Thus a child A says he has a brother B, but A says B has no brother. Similarly, others can be enemies or foreigners, but rarely the self in relation to others.

Within these limitations, and as age advances, feelings can be discussed with language appropriate to the age-group. This point makes the discussion of moral issues with large age-ranges, such as at school assemblies, particularly fruitless, as the language cannot be suitable for all. The actual changing of attitudes by discussion of moral issues has been shown, as in the case of the discussions of films, to be reasonably well-established (19) (21). With the young, however, the teacher has to prompt, as children cannot stand back and view issues objectively as we sometimes think (16).

j. **Pupil participation.**

Historically, the demands of students for a greater say in the running of universities and colleges can hardly be described as new or revolutionary. In the Middle Ages professors were elected by students and the *studium generale* existed primarily for, and, insofar as administration was required, was run by, the students themselves. The more persistent demands have been at the higher educational level and outside Britain, although there have been signs that demands will grow in this country too. It is interesting to note that the more violent actions and extreme demands occur where the rigidity of teaching and examination, and the principles of selection are most severe, and where the degree of personal contact students have with the staff is small.

If the adolescent is to be responsible, he must feel he is really being taught; that there are many worthwhile things to do; that his opinions and feelings count; that the school or college recognises the status he wishes to have, and often does have, outside the academic walls; that school or college has some bearing on what he will do when he leaves (1). Since the break with conventional morality is said to occur at about 14 years of age, there are strong arguments for the raising of the transfer age to about that age (as it is in preparatory and public schools). The advantage would then be that concentration would then be possible on the creation of different atmospheres in the schools. The school for the younger would encourage questioning within a conventional framework and with more rules surrounding its administration. The other would encourage a more mature and individualistic atmosphere, requiring less adherence to rules and more rational justification of actions which are contrary to the wishes of authority or the majority of pupils. Such a school would wish to set standards, though, as always, of not too black-and-white a kind in order to avoid setting up conflict when expectations are not reached (2). When the children are allowed to give opinions they will be more inclined to feel that within the limits of the system they have been allowed to have their say and, at the same time, can be made aware of the shortcomings of their arguments, sometimes by fellow-pupils. Despite odd differences of opinions, they can and should be made to feel they can identify themselves with the aims of the school.

The Newsom Report comments:

'History and geography, literature, civics and science, all play their part in forming the moral outlook of boys and girls . . . through these subjects the whole staff, irrespective of religious affiliation, can make a contribution to both the spiritual and moral development of the pupils.'

Many believe that this pious aspiration will never be fully achieved until we all share the same values; clearly until that day

arrives we must do our best to give to children
    'the habitual vision of greatness'
which Whitehead believed to be
    'essential to moral development.'

Summary

4.*1*–**4.***9*

    The teacher's role has to be considered in conjunction with that of the parent, and constant contact between the two is essential if they are to work in harmony. The teacher with the greatest influence over his pupils is likely to be the one who allows the formation of groups, takes a personal interest in each child and has wide interests. By doing this his authoritative position is not necessarily weakened, although it is the greatest test of teacher-effectiveness.

    The following 10 points are suggested as aims (24):   **4.***10*

1. The pupil's need for a secure framework in terms of a group-identity.
2. His need for a personal identity in terms of feeling confident, successful, useful, and wanted, particularly in the case of underprivileged children.
3. The importance of close personal contact with adults.
4. His ability to develop moral concepts, and to communicate linguistically.
5. The relevance of rule-governed activities and contracts.
6. The importance of parent-figures and of a firm and clearly-defined authority.
7. The need to channel or institutionalize aggression.
8. The merits of cooperation as against competition.
9. The need to enable the pupil to objectify his own feelings.
10. The importance of getting the pupil to participate, and to make the educational situation 'come alive'.

Questions for Discussion

1. Is the home or the school the more important agency for moral education, and what precisely should the school aim to do?

2. Is teaching moral values a different task from teaching school subjects?

3. Select and discuss some themes from literature, history or contemporary life which could provide the basis for moral education.

4. Considering the historical change in the role of the teacher, is he now in a better or worse position for leading discussion on moral issues?

5. What impact do you think school reorganization and curriculum changes are likely to have in the sphere of values?

Bibliography

(1)
Allen, E. A. **Attitudes of Children and Adolescents in School.**
Educational Research, 3, 65–80, 1960.

(2)
Allinsmith, W. **Conscience and Conflict: The Moral Force in Personality.**
Child Development, 28, 469—76, 1957.

(3)
Allinsmith, W. **Moral Standards: The Learning of Moral Standards** *in Inner Conflict and Defense*
ed. D. R. Miller and G. E. Swainson.
New York: Holt, 1960.

(4)
Aronfreed, J. **Internal and external orientation in the moral behaviour of children.**
Paper read at the meeting of the American Psychological Association, Cincinatti, Ohio September, 1960.

(5)
Bernstein, B. **Social Structure, Language and Learning** *in Linking Home and School,*
ed. Maurice Croft et al. London: Longmans, 1967.

(6)
Brearley, M. **A Teacher's Guide to Reading Piaget**
Hitchfield, E. *London: Routledge and Kegan Paul, 1966.*

(7)
Dolger, L.
Grinandes, J.
Children's Attitude towards Discipline as related to Socioeconomic status.
J. Experimental Education, 15, 161–5, 1946.

(8)
Evans, K. M.
Attitudes and Interests in Education
London: Routledge and Kegan Paul, 1965.

(9)
Flanders, N. A.
Some Relationships Among Teacher Influence, Pupil Attitudes and Achievement *in Contemporary Research on Teacher Effectiveness, ed. B. J. Biddle and W. J. Ellena, New York: Rinehart and Winston, 1960.*

(10)
Floud, J. E.
Teaching in the Affluent Society.
Br. J. Sociol., 13, 299–308, 1962.

(11)
Gladstone, R.
Do Maladjusted Teachers cause Maladjustment? A re-review.
J. except. Child., 15, 65–70, 1948.

(12)
Hollis, A. W.
The Personal Relationship in Teaching.
Unpublished M. A. thesis. University o Birmingham Library, 1935.

(13)
Hourd, M.
The Education of the Poetic Spirit.
London: Heinemann, 1949.

(14)

Lewin, K. **Patterns of Aggressive Behaviour**
Lippitt, R. **in Experimentally created Social**
White, R. K. **Climates.**
J. Soc. Psychol., 10, 271–99, 1931.

(15)

Low-Beer, A. **Moral Judgments in History and**
History Teaching *in the Nature of History*
and History Teaching, ed. W. H. Burston
and D. Thompson.
London: Routledge and Kegan Paul, 1967.

(16)

McNaughton, A. **Piaget's Theory and Primary School**
Social Studies.
Educational Review, 19, 23–32, 1966.

(17)

Morris, B. **Studies in Education** *No.* 7.
London: Evans, 1955.

(18)

Piaget, J. **Judgement and Reasoning in the Child.**
London: Routledge, 1928.

(19)

Rosen I. C. **The Effect of the Motion Picture**
Gentlemen's Agreement on Attitudes
towards Jews.
J. Psychol. 26, 525–36, 1948.

(20)

Storr, A. **Human Aggression.**
Penguin Books, 1968.

(21)

Thurstone, L. L. **Influence of Motion Pictures on Children's Attitudes.** *J. Soc. Psychol. 2, 291–305, 1931.*

(22)

Tudhope, W. **Motives for the Choice of the Teaching Profession by Training College Students.** *Brit. J. Educ. Psychol., 14, 129–41, 1944.*

(23)

Whiting, J. W. M. **Child Training and Personality.** Child, I. *New Haven: Yale University Press, 1953.*

(24)

Wilson, J. **Introduction to Moral Education.** Williams, N. *Penguin Books, 1968.* Sugarman, B.

(25)

Zucker, H. J. **Affectional Identifications and Delinquency.** *Archives of Psychol., No. 286, 1943.*